KALEIDOSCOPE

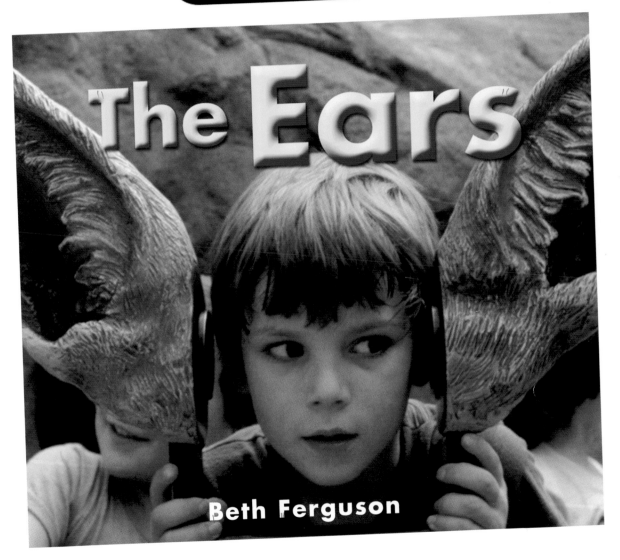

The Ears

Beth Ferguson

BENCHMARK BOOKS

MARSHALL CAVENDISH
NEW YORK

Benchmark Books
Marshall Cavendish
99 White Plains Road
Tarrytown, NY 10591
www.marshallcavendish.com

Library of Congress Cataloging-in-Publication Data

Ferguson, Beth, 1968–
    The Ears / by Beth Ferguson.
        v. cm. — (Kaleidoscope)
    Includes bibliographical references and index.
    Contents: Ears are for hearing — What is sound? — How your ears hear
— Balancing your body — When ears need help — Keeping ears healthy.
    ISBN 0-7614-1592-0
    1. Ear—Juvenile literature. 2. Hearing—Juvenile literature. [1.
Ear. 2. Hearing. 3. Senses and sensation.] I. Title. II. Series:
Kaleidoscope (Tarrytown, N.Y.)
    QP462.2.F47 2004   612.8'5—dc21
                                                                2003000651

Photo research by Anne Burns Images

Cover photo: Photo Researchers, Inc./Saturn Stills/Science Photo Library

The photographs in this book are used with permission and through the courtesy of:
Corbis: Jacques Chenet, title page; Royalty Free, 4; 11; Russell Munson, 16; Richard Cummins, 28; Jonathan Torgovnik,
31; LWA Dann Tardif, 39; Lawrence Manning, 40. *Superstock:* 7, 35. *Custom Medical Stock Photo:* 8, 24, 36. *Photo
Researchers, Inc./Science Photo Library:* Martin Dohrn, 12; David Gifford, 15; Dave Roberts, 19; John Bavosi, 20; Dr.
G. Oran Bredberg, 23; Kairos/Latin Stock, 32; Will & Deni McIntyre, 43. *Cajun Images:* Charles Martin, 27.

Series design by Adam Mietlowski

Printed in Italy

6 5 4 3 2 1

Contents

Ears Are for Hearing

Think of all the ways you use your ears every day. You wake up to a loud alarm clock. At breakfast, you listen closely while your dad tells you a funny story. As you wait for the school bus, you hear a bird singing. All these sounds help you make sense of the world around you. It's hard to imagine what life would be like if you couldn't hear.

According to Helen Keller, a famous woman who was both blind and deaf, "The problems of deafness are deeper and more complex, if not more important, than those of blindness. Deafness is a much worse misfortune."

Your ears help you in countless ways. They allow you to hear the conversation at the breakfast table.

What Is Sound?

When you throw a rock into the quiet waters of a pond, you can see tiny waves ripple out in all directions. The same thing happens whenever a bell rings, a car horn blasts, or a child coughs. **Sound waves** reach out from the source of the noise. When those waves strike your head, your ears **amplify** the sound and send messages to your brain. Then nerve cells in your brain decode and interpret the sound messages. This process is called hearing.

Sound waves move outward in all directions just like these ripples in the water. ▶

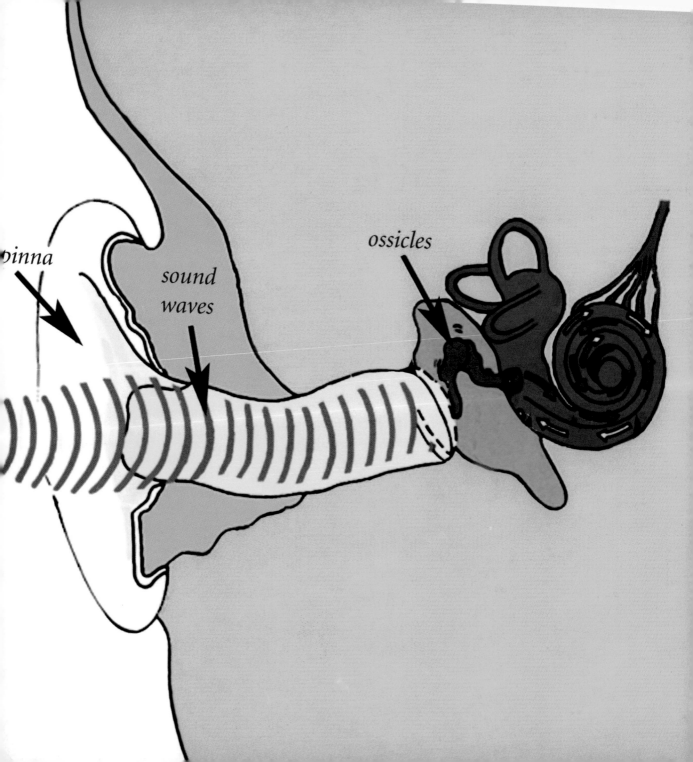

What can sound waves tell you? More than you might think. The taller the wave, the louder the sound. Scientists measure the loudness of a sound in decibels (dB). A whisper measures about 20 dB, while a normal speaking voice is around 60 dB. Any sound above 100 dB can damage your ears. Because rock concerts may reach 130 dB, many musicians lose some of their hearing.

The **frequency** of sound waves determines the **pitch** of the sound. The waves made by high-pitched noises, such as a scream or a whistle, have a high frequency. They are closer together than the ones made by crashing thunder, snoring, and other low-pitched noises. Scientists measure pitch in hertz (Hz). Most children can hear sounds with pitches between 20 and 20,000 Hz. But as people get older, they often lose their ability to hear high-pitched and low-pitched sounds.

◁ *An illustration of how sound waves travel through the ear*

Because you have two ears—one on either side of your head—your brain can tell where sound waves are coming from. For example, once your brain has identified a high-pitched sound as an ambulance siren, it is important to know where the ambulance is. Will your mom have to pull over and let it pass? If your left ear collects taller sound waves than your right ear, your brain will know that the ambulance is to your left. And since the sound waves are getting taller and taller, your brain knows the ambulance is moving toward you. Even though you can't see the ambulance yet, you know it is driving up the side street to your left.

Each of your ears gathers sound waves. If you're listening to music, for example, they combine the waves to create a full, rich sound.

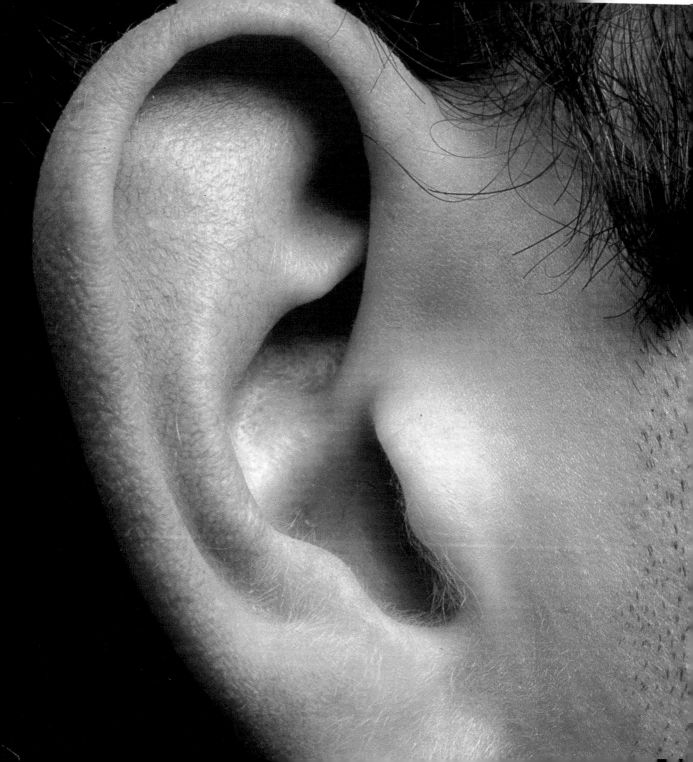

Most of the sound waves that reach your ear are collected by your outer ear, or **pinna**. But a few reach your inner ear by traveling through the bones in your head. Your voice sounds richer and deeper to you than it does to other people because you hear sound waves from both sources. To hear how your voice sounds to other people, talk into a tape recorder. When you play back the tape, you will hear only sound waves collected by your pinna.

◀ *A person's outer ear, or pinna, collects sounds waves and funnels them to the eardrum.*

How Your Ears Hear

When you look at your ear in the mirror, all you can see is your pinna. The top of your pinna is made of flexible **cartilage.** The soft lobe at the bottom contains fat. The rest of your ear is located inside your head. It is surrounded by thick, heavy bone that protects it from injuries.

Your **auditory canal** is the tube that leads from your pinna to your **eardrum.** It is a little more than 1 inch (2.5 centimeters) long and is lined with tiny, bristly hairs. Small **glands** surrounding the canal produce earwax. This yellow, sticky material traps tiny bits of dust and dirt that get into your ear.

Your eardrum is a thin, circular **membrane** that stretches across the far end of the auditory canal. When sound waves strike your eardrum, it shakes, or **vibrates.** The vibrations

Your auditory canal connects your outer ear and your eardrum.   ▶

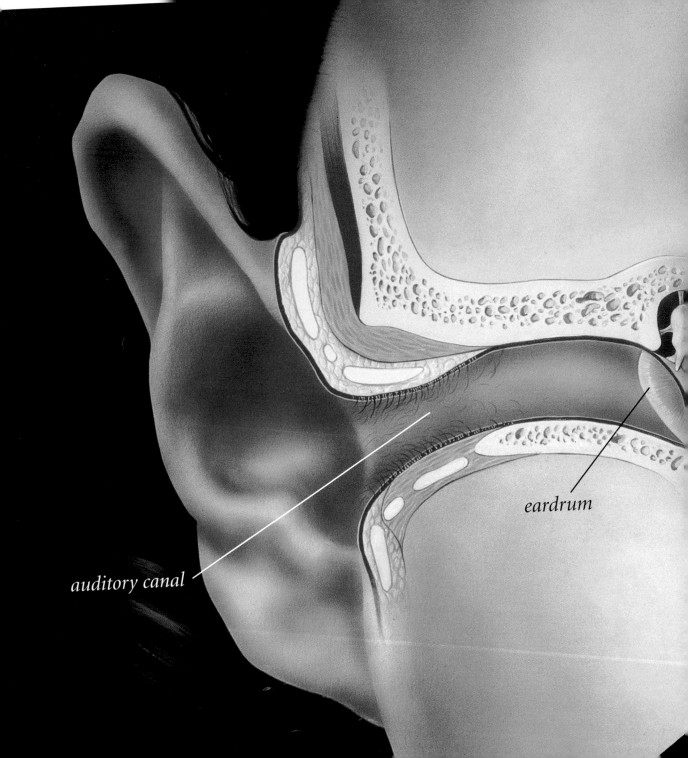

auditory canal

eardrum

move through three tiny bones in your middle ear. The middle ear is like a tiny room, with the eardrum at one end and another membrane called the **oval window** at the other. A hole in the "floor" of the middle ear leads to the **eustachian tube**—a channel that extends into the back of the throat. It allows air to move in and out of your middle ear, so the air pressure on both sides of your eardrum stays the same.

If you drive up a mountain or take off in an airplane, the air pressure around you decreases rapidly. Each time you swallow or yawn, the opening of your eustachian tube will widen. Your ears will "pop" because the wider opening allows large quantities of lower-pressure air to race up your eustachian tube, while higher-pressure air zooms toward your throat.

When you take off in an airplane, the air pressure around your body decreases very quickly. You may need to swallow or chew gum, so your eustachian tube opens wide enough to let air with a lower pressure into your middle ear.

When you have a cold, parts of your nose may swell up and block your eustachian tube. This makes it difficult for air to move in and out of your middle ear. If you fly while you are sick, you may feel a sharp pain inside your ears. During takeoff, the air pressure in your auditory canal decreases, but the air pressure in your middle ear does not change. The high-pressure air trapped in your middle ear pushes against your eardrum and stretches it. This can be very painful.

Even after the airplane lands, you may have trouble hearing for a while. Your eardrum must return to its normal shape before it can work properly.

Your eardrum transfers sound vibrations to the **hammer** —a tiny bone connected to the eardrum. The hammer rests against the **anvil**, which touches the **stirrup**. The hammer, anvil, and stirrup are the three smallest bones in the body. Together they amplify sound vibrations collected by your pinna.

Also called the ossicles, the hammer, anvil, and stirrup are the tiniest bones in the human body.

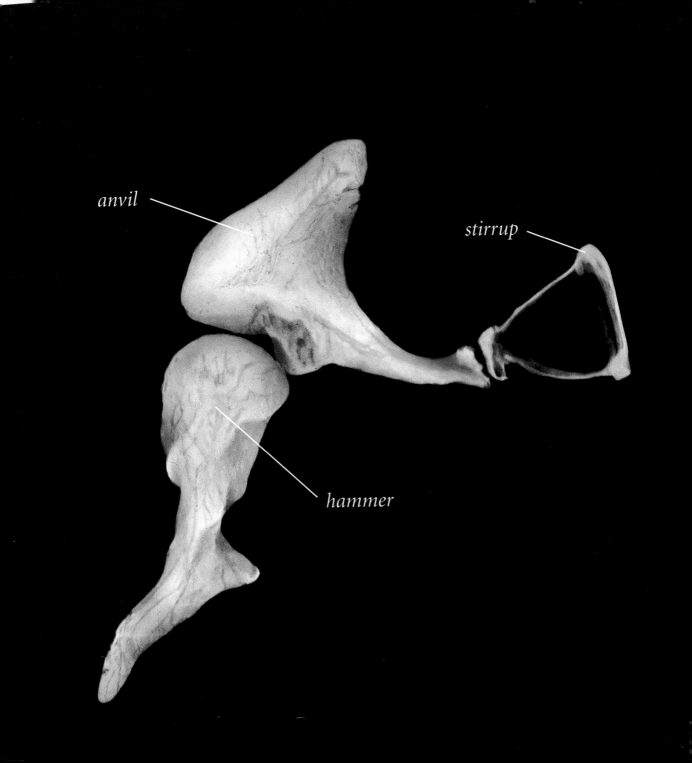

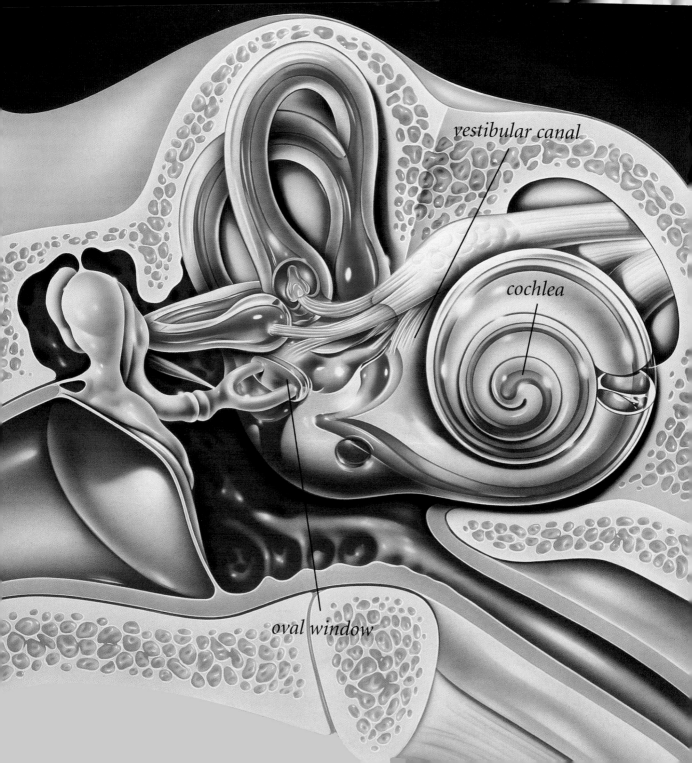

vestibular canal

cochlea

oval window

The stirrup rests against the oval window, the membrane that separates the middle ear from the inner ear. Sound vibrations force the end of the stirrup to push against and then pull away from the oval window. This movement causes fluid inside the cochlea to form waves. The **cochlea**, a snail-shaped structure about the size of your fingertip, is divided into three parts.

First, the waves move through the cochlea's **vestibular canal**. When they reach the center of the spiral, the waves pass into the **tympanic canal**. They continue to travel outward until they reach the **round window**. The waves cause the round window to bulge in and out until their energy passes out of the ear.

From the outside, the spiraling cochlea looks like a snail's shell.

Between the vestibular canal and the tympanic canal is the **cochlear canal**. This is where hearing takes place. Inside the cochlear canal is a structure called the **organ of Corti**. It is lined with more than 20,000 hearing cells. As waves of fluid brush against the sensitive hairs at the top of each hearing cell, sound messages are sent to the **auditory nerve**, which runs along the bases of the hearing cells. The auditory nerve then carries these sound signals to the brain.

This photograph of the organ of Corti (blue) was taken through a high-power microscope. It shows the sensitive hairs (yellow) at the top of some hearing cells (red).

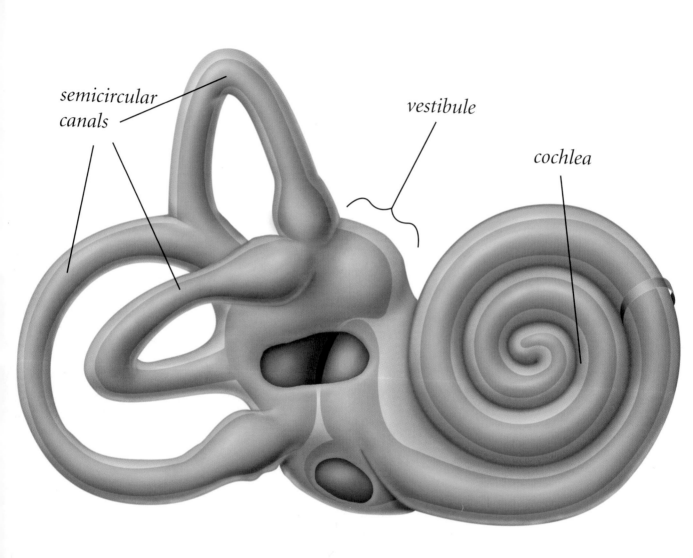

semicircular canals

vestibule

cochlea

Balancing Your Body

The auditory nerve also carries other kinds of messages to your brain. Some of these messages come from the **vestibule**, which is attached to the cochlea. The vestibule contains two small sacs. Each one is lined with sensitive hairs and filled with a jellylike material that contains tiny, solid crystals.

When you hold your head upright, the crystals inside each sac are spread out evenly. But if you move your head, **gravity** causes the crystals to slide through the jelly to the lowest area of each sac. Then the hairs along that side of the sac send out nerve signals, so your brain always knows the position of your head.

◄ *This drawing of the inner ear shows the semicircular canals, the vestibule, and the cochlea.*

A different set of messages comes from the three loop-shaped **semicircular canals** located above the vestibule. These messages give your brain information about the position and movement of your entire body, so you won't lose your balance. When you turn around, lie down, or stand on your head, fluid in the semicircular canals flows in the direction of the movement, causing sensitive hairs at the base of each canal to bend. The motion of the hairs sends messages to your brain. In response, your brain sends more signals to your muscles, so you will not fall over.

When you stand on your head, your semicircular canals go to work. They send messages to your brain, so you won't fall over.

Sometimes your brain receives opposing messages from different parts of your body. For example, if you spin in circles and then stop suddenly, you will feel very dizzy. You may even fall over. Even though your body is at rest, the fluid in your semicircular canals is still moving, so your brain thinks your whole body is still spinning. The same thing can happen after you ride a merry-go-round.

Have you ever felt sick to your stomach while riding in a car? Car sickness occurs when your eyes and ears send different messages to your brain. When you ride in a car, your seat belt prevents you from moving around. Your semicircular canals tell your brain you are sitting still, but your eyes tell your brain that you are moving. To prevent car sickness, look straight ahead at the horizon so your eyes will send the same message as your ears.

After the ride on this merry-go-round is over, the fluid in this boy's semicircular canals will still be sloshing around. His brain will think he is still in motion.

When Ears Need Help

Even though most people depend on their ears to understand their surroundings, not everyone has perfect hearing. As people get older, their eardrums often become harder and thicker. As a result, they have trouble hearing high-pitched and low-pitched sounds.

Loud noises can also harm your ears. Everyone hears loud noises from time to time. When very tall sound waves enter your pinna, a group of muscles tightens the eardrum. This reduces the vibrations that pass along the hammer, anvil, and stirrup. At the same time, another group of muscles moves the stirrup farther from the oval window. This limits the impact the vibrations have on the fluid inside the cochlea.

A loud sound such as a scream can do serious damage to your ears. ▶

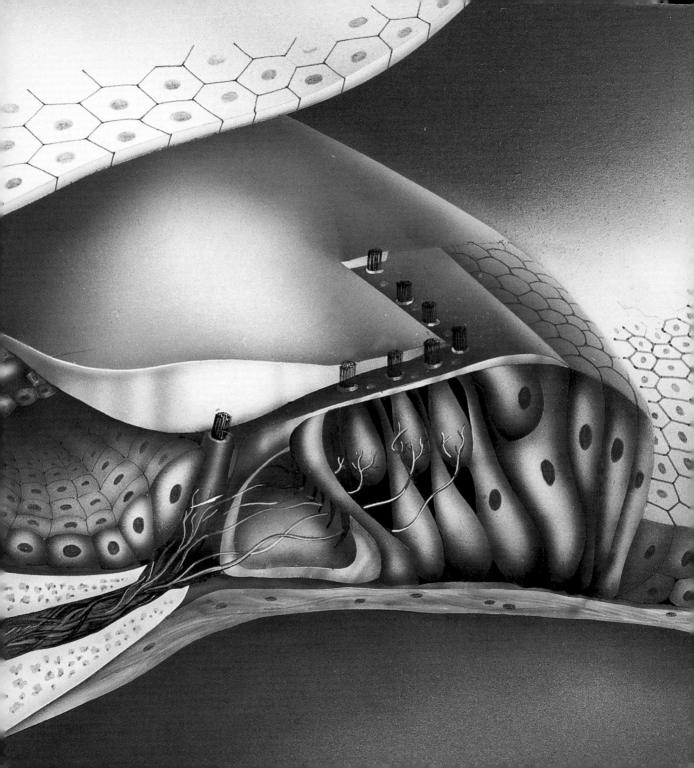

But when people hear loud noises for several hours at a time or day after day, their ears begin to have trouble protecting their delicate parts. The louder a noise is, the more it bends the hairs that line the organ of Corti. If these sensitive hairs are bent too long or too much, they will not be able to recover. If you ever hear ringing in your ears, it might be a warning. It means some of the hairs inside your organ of Corti have been permanently damaged.

The hairs that line the organ of Corti are flexible and very sensitive. If they are bent too much, they may become damaged. Your hearing may suffer as a result.

While there is no way to repair damaged hairs, many hearing problems can be improved with a **hearing aid**. A hearing aid is a tiny device that contains a microphone, an amplifier, and a loudspeaker. It increases the size of the sound waves, so messages can be sent to the brain even if the eardrum or some areas of the middle ear do not work properly.

Many conditions can affect your ears for a short time. One of the most common illnesses that affects children is middle ear infections. More than 10 million children are treated for ear infections every year. Doctors estimate that nearly 90 percent of all American children have had at least one middle ear infection by the time they are seven years old.

A hearing aid fits snugly inside a person's outer ear.

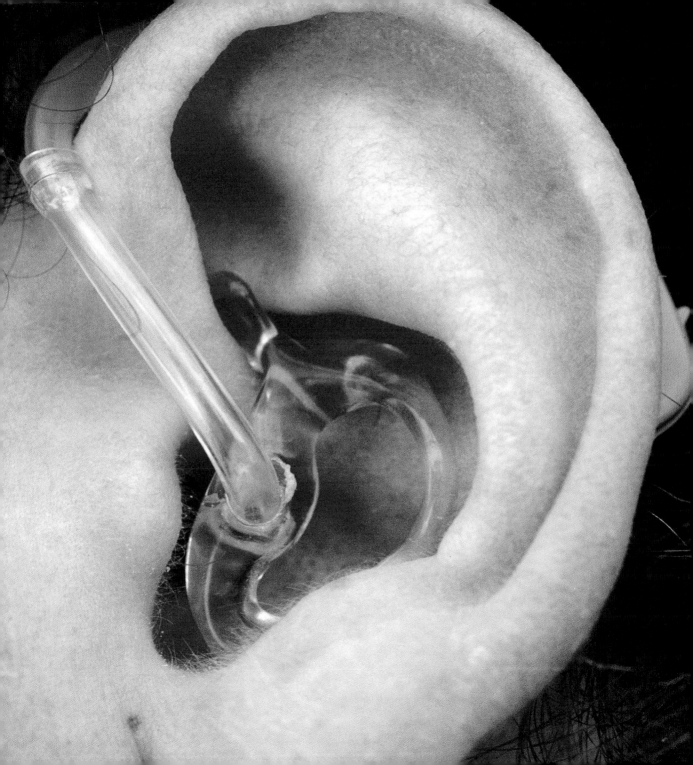

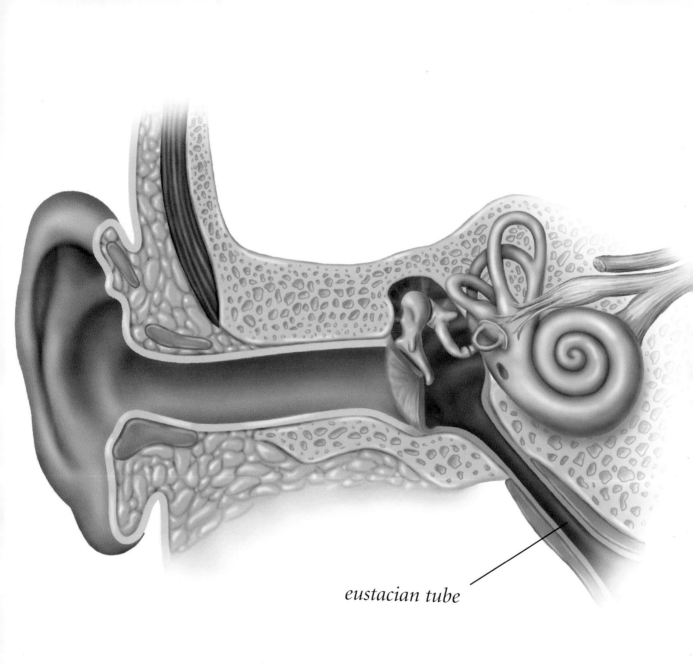

eustacian tube

Many children's eustachian tubes are shaped in a way that makes it easy for cold germs to travel into their ears. If the inside of a child's nose swells up, fluid and germs may be trapped in the ear. As material builds up inside the middle ear, a painful infection may develop. Because the tiny bones in the middle ear may have trouble moving, the child may have trouble hearing clearly.

Ear infections can occur when germs travel up the eustachian tube and into the middle ear.

Most ear infections either get better by themselves or can be treated with medicine. But if a child has ear infections over and over, a doctor may want to put tubes in his or her ears. During a short operation, the doctor makes a small slit in the eardrum and puts in a little tube that helps drain fluid and germs out of the middle ear.

There isn't much you can do to prevent middle ear infections, but blowing your nose gently can help. Powerful blows may push unwanted germs into your ears.

This little girl is having her ears checked by a doctor. Regular ear exams are a must. ▷

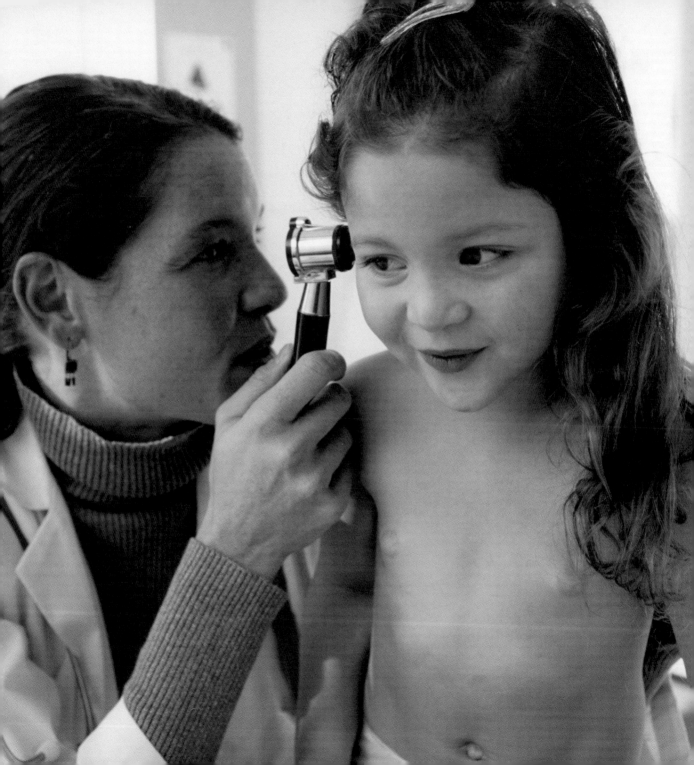

Keeping Ears Healthy

There are many other things you can do to keep your ears healthy. Never poke sharp objects into your ear. You wouldn't want to accidentally make a hole in your eardrum. If earwax builds up in your auditory canal, it is best to let a doctor remove it.

Since loud sounds can cause hearing loss, think about the noises around you every day. Workers who use heavy machinery often wear earplugs to protect their ears. It might be a good idea for you to wear them when you mow the lawn, vacuum, or go to a concert. You should also be careful when you listen to music at home. Keep the volume low, especially if you are wearing headphones.

◀ *Loud music can damage your ears, so turn down the volume.*

Sometimes it takes people a while to realize that they have a hearing problem. Even though your school has probably tested your hearing, it's a good idea to have your doctor check it again at your annual exam. If the doctor thinks there might be a problem, he or she might suggest that you visit a specialist.

One of the best ways to help your ears is to take good care of the rest of your body. Eat plenty of healthful foods and avoid sweets. Run, play, and have fun with your friends during the day. At night, get plenty of sleep. If you do all these things, your body will make sure that your ears are always in tip-top shape.

Do you hear what I hear? Your ears are incredible organs and need to be cared for like the rest of your body.

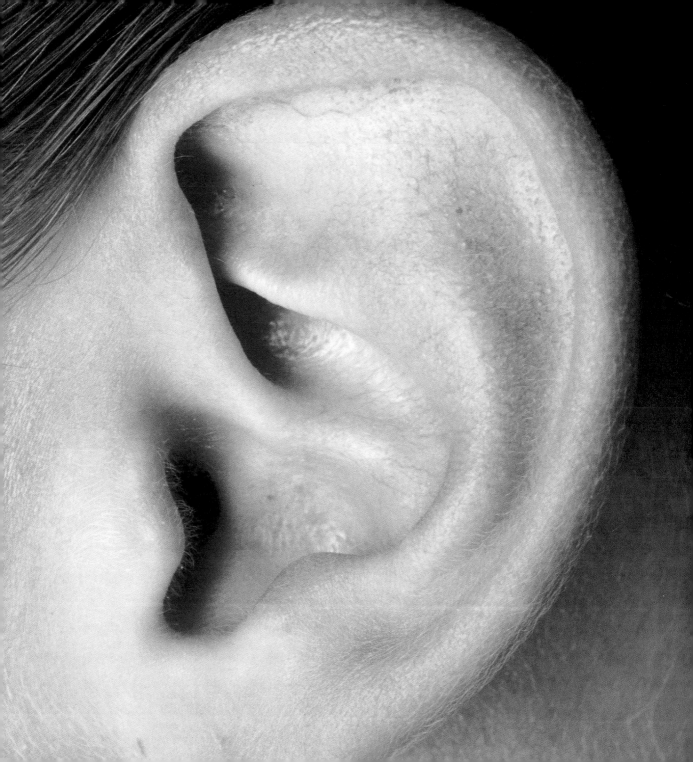

Glossary

amplify—To increase or make larger.

anvil—One of the three tiny bones in the middle ear. It is shaped like the anvil blacksmiths once used to make horseshoes and other metal items.

auditory canal—The tube that leads from the pinna to the eardrum.

auditory nerve—The cord that carries messages from the inner ear to the brain. It transports sound messages from the organ of Corti and messages about position and balance from the vestibule and semicircular canals.

cartilage—The flexible material that gives your nose and outer ears their shape.

cochlea—A coiling, snail-shaped structure in the inner ear. It is filled with fluid that creates the waves that bend the hairs in the organ of Corti.

cochlear canal—One of the three canals in the cochlea. It houses the organ of Corti and the auditory nerve.

eardrum—The membrane that separates the outer ear from the middle ear. It vibrates when sound waves hit it.

eustachian tube—A tube that connects the middle ear to the back of the throat. It allows air to flow in and out of the middle ear.

frequency—How often something happens in a given amount of time. It is used to describe the number of sound waves that pass a person's ear during a set amount of time.

gland—A tiny body part that produces and releases materials, such as earwax.

gravity—A force that makes objects on or near Earth fall toward the center of the planet.

hammer—One of the tiny bones in the middle ear. It fits into the eardrum and gets its name from its shape.

hearing aid—A device that fits in the auditory canal and amplifies sound waves.

membrane—A thin sheet of tissue.

oval window—The membrane that separates the middle ear from the inner ear. When the stirrup strikes the oval window, it moves the fluid inside the cochlea.

organ of Corti—A structure inside the cochlear canal that contains hearing cells.

pinna—The outer ear.

pitch—A quality of sound caused by the frequency of the waves.

round window—A membrane that releases sound energy from the ear.

semicircular canal—One of the three loop-shaped structures in the inner ear. The semicircular canals detect changes in the position of the body, so the brain can direct muscles to maintain balance.

sound wave—The form sound energy takes as it moves through solids, liquids, and gases.

stirrup—The smallest bone in the human body. It is shaped like the stirrup, or footrest, that hangs down from a horse's saddle. When the anvil strikes the stirrup, the bottom of the bone strikes the oval window.

tympanic canal—One of the canals in the cochlea. It carries waves it received from the vestibular canal to the round window.

vestibular canal—One of the canals in the cochlea. As the oval window pushes into the fluid-filled vestibular canal, waves form.

vestibule—A structure in the inner ear. It contains two small sacs that sense changes in the position of the head.

vibrate—To shake.

Find Out More

Books

Ballard, Carol. *How Do Our Ears Hear?* Austin, TX: Raintree Steck-Vaughn, 1998.

Cobb, Vicki. *Perk Up Your Ears: Discover Your Sense of Hearing.* Brookfield, CT: Millbrook Press, 2001.

Dooley, Virginia. *Tubes in My Ears: My Trip to the Hospital.* Greenvale, NY: Mondo, 1996.

Gibson, Gary. *Hearing Sounds.* Brookfield, CT: Copper Beech Books, 1995.

Goode, Katherine. *Ears.* Woodbridge, CT: Blackbirch Press, 2000.

Hurwitz, Sue. *Hearing.* Danbury, CT: Franklin Watts, 1999.

Pringle, Laurence. *Hearing.* Tarrytown, NY: Benchmark Books, 1999.

Organizations and Online Sites

Hearing Alliance of America
http://hearingalliance.com
P.O. Box 4084
Torrance, CA 90510

House Ear Institute
http://hei.org
2100 W. 3rd St.
Los Angeles, CA 90057

Questions and Answers: Information About Your Hearing
http://www.nidcd.nih.gov/health/education/owlgame/owl.html
How much do you really know about your ears? Take this quick quiz
created just for kids.

Author's Bio

Beth Ferguson earned a bachelor's degree in biology from Union College
and a master's degree in science and environmental journalism from
New York University. After working as an editor for many years, she now
writes about science and medicine. Ms. Ferguson lives in Massachusetts.

Index